NERVES
OF
STEEL

NERVES OF STEEL

LESSONS THAT MS TAUGHT ME

TRACE J. SHERER

WITH **CANDI S. CROSS**

To my mother, Barbara, whose delightful and wicked
sense of humor and compassion shaped the person I am.

Praise for NERVES OF STEEL

"There is so much that can be revealed about ourselves when we take the time to see life from another perspective. Within pages of starting Nerves of Steel, *I was reminded of not only the power, but also, the joy that my choices can create. Admittedly, I've been feeling overwhelmed by the choices available to me, which has led me to a sort of mental and emotional paralysis. I know that it's a paralysis of my own doing. Enter Trace Sherer, a stranger to me by all definitions of the word, to offer me a glimmer of light back to who I know myself to be. I firmly believe readers will find motivation in his story, not because of the successes he shares, but because of the challenges he made his way through to achieve them."*

—Antuan Magic Raimone,
TEDx Speaker, Hamilton *Universal Swing, Author of* Becoming Magic: A Path of Personal Reconstruction

"This book grabs your attention from the first paragraph. Trace brings uplifting teachings to address issues that all of us face at some point in our lives. If you are in search of real-world solutions to real-world challenges, this book is for you. Through his life of overcoming obstacles, Trace provides a blueprint to follow that will most certainly bring happiness and success. I haven't read anything like this before. His story is unique and should be read by anyone who is seeking a better direction in life."

—Randy Sorrels,
Attorney, President State Bar of Texas 2019-2020

"Trace's ability to use positivity in the hardest situations speaks to the power of mindset. In medical practice we often see the most positive patients thrive in the face of death, and his story is a testament to that! His story spreads hope and light and is worth the read for anyone dealing with an unexpected, life-altering challenge."

—Danielle DonDiego, DO, MBA,
Author of Self-Care RX

"Following the murder of my daughter, I quickly learned about perspective and perseverance. Life is full of amazing people who show us every day that the perspective we put on our lives, combined with amazing perseverance, makes us capable of amazing things. For Trace, it has meant the difference between life and death. Trace teaches us all lessons about going forward from horrible news and determining our own outcomes. In spite of a death sentence due to illness back in 1999, he is able to write today that he is grateful to be alive. His choice to be positive is a lesson for us all as we go forward from our own moments in life."

—Fred Guttenberg,
Speaker and Author of Find the Helpers

"*Nerves of Steel is poignant and funny. Trace's ability to open up to us and weave his story, while reminding us that happiness and positivity are a choice, is a testament to his own strength and tenacity. Mindset shapes reality.* Nerves of Steel *is a reminder that with awareness, love and finding your tribe, you can tackle your health and your life and come out on top.*"

—*Sharon Holand Gelfand,*
Functional, Holistic Nutritionist and Author of
The G.U.T. Method

"*Trace Sherer is definitely a positive force of nature. Who else would feel grateful to be alive during the past year of pandemic, racial injustice, riots and protest? 'Positivity,' he says, 'is the only way for me.' This approach not only helped Trace flourish and thrive; he wrote this book when others were paralyzed by fear and hopelessness. Trace's unrelenting positivity has fueled him to still be alive more than 20 years after a doctor gave him two years to live, following an MS diagnosis! More people should adopt Trace's approach to life. To learn about it, read his uplifting book,* Nerves of Steel: Lessons That MS Taught Me.*"

—*Patrice Tanaka,*
Founder & Chief Joy Officer, Joyful Planet LLC

"*Trace, in* Nerves of Steel, *is so honest. Having lived with a chronic, long undiagnosed illness myself for most of my adult life, I know his assertions of positive thinking are right on target. We must not—cannot—give up. Turning challenges into positives have been the biggest gifts of my life and I can see a lot of Trace in me. I bet you will, too. Most of us are hardest on ourselves, which is why we must follow his advice to find our tribe and keep moving forward toward the good things life has to offer. No matter how bleak things may seem, there is always hope. Kudos to Trace for his honesty and clear voice. This is a book anyone faced with a major health or life challenge should read without delay.*"

—*Adriana Jaymes,*
Author of Running from Bears

"*In* Nerves of SteeI, *Trace reminds us that we have a choice. That we always have a choice to control our own thoughts. With compassion and wit, he takes us through his process. He gives us a glimpse behind the curtain of how he has played the hands that life has dealt him. His tale is a love story, about his love of life, simply not to be missed. And as for 'dreaming out loud', he has convinced me that there's so much to gain from it.*"

—*Fran Macferran,*
President and CEO, Hobby Center for Performing Arts

CONTENTS

ACKNOWLEDGEMENTS

My family is solid gold! My sons, Trevor and Preston; my brother-in-law, Michael; sister, Kimi, who pushed me to tell my story and found the top-notch collaborator who would see it through; and brother from another mother, Mush Khan.

Dr. Igor Cherches, Lynn Maki, and all my healthcare providers, for years of stellar care and wrapping me up in hope while keeping it real.

Team Inspiration-Texas: Nathan Beedle (and my bad right leg, "Jarvis," which he aptly named), Jim Harrington, Trisha Bicknell, Scott Riddle, Brandon Loughridge, and Tyler Blanton.

Richard Hubscher, who has cared for my pets and me in so many ways, thank you!

I'm eternally grateful for my friend, collaborative writer, and editor, Candi Cross, whose skills, dedication, and passion *are* the nerves of steel that helped bring my story to life.

Thank you to those who have reached out to me from all over the world from as far away as Melbourne, Australia in response to my random thoughts (you know who you are!); your positive insights and smiles made so many of my days. Finally, to every person who has faced a challenge that they thought was insurmountable—it isn't. This book is for you.

POSITIVITY IS POWER

"Correction does much, but encouragement does more."

—Johann Wolfgang von Goethe

A FRIEND ASKED ME how on earth I could possibly stay positive with all of the uncertainty in the world today. The pandemic, racial injustice, riots, protests. Not to mention rarer, but very real, events of nature like the invasion of murder hornets, the puppy born with green fur, lions napping on a highway during quarantine, and jellyfish as big as dinner plates scattered along our shores. Who would want to miss out on these once-in-a-lifetime moments? I'm so grateful to be *alive* for these moments. And positivity is the only way for me. Especially right now. I've had a lot of time to think lately and that decision to stay positive is the only reason that I am functioning. I have no choice. I must stay positive.

In 1999, I was diagnosed with multiple sclerosis (MS) and told in the sternest voice during a second opinion that I would be in a wheelchair by the end of 1999 and dead by 2001. My first thought was that my kids are little—I'm not "doing this" to them. Honestly, who wants to sit around waiting to die because someone basically prescribed it? Don't get me wrong; I have always respected doctors a great deal, but they're people, too. As such, they could never predict my outcome if I fought this disease and flooded my cells with positivity. Of course, there would be pain, setbacks, stressful life changes, and physical deterioration. However, I would also make sure of gratifying experiences, kindness, achievement, resilience, and joy. Don't ever underestimate the healing power of incredible moments.

I went back to my original doctor who aligned with my thought process and determination. He approached this diagnosis with a very different attitude than the doom messenger. He was willing to fight, too, and forge a way to help me maintain my best health along this journey. I truly felt that I found the best match for me and my grit.

I have also realized how important this lesson from my parents really is: Any situation we are in gives us the ability to choose a path. We can either deal with it in a positive manner or allow the negative things in our lives to defeat us. I refuse to allow that to happen. My parents always made us realize that we cannot change the hand that we are dealt, but rather, we are defined by how we choose to approach and deal with challenges. Life is supposed to be lived happily. I want to find the avenue that allows me to live a happy life. Sometimes it is extremely difficult. Sometimes it feels like it is impossible. But we have to.

Happiness shines through the darkest times if you summon it. I'll give you a lighthearted example, and I hope my feisty mother will forgive me from heaven for it. As my mother's time on this earth was coming to a close, my son, Trevor, came into town to see her. She woke up that morning and asked her caregiver to do her hair and give her a full face of makeup. She was so excited and wanted to solve the world's problems with a little merriment. She was an occasional social drinker with fun, colorful drinks. It's absolutely hysterical when your eighty-nine-year-old mother *insists* on doing a shot at 11:00 in the morning with everyone—and with a broad smile. (For the record, we did a shot of water and didn't tell her it was only water.) Life is good! *This* is how a Sherer handles organ failure. There are countless examples of how she handled life's missiles with grace and grit. How could I ever let my mom down by having nerves of mush? (No offense, Mush!)

CONFESSIONS OF AN OPPORTUNITY-FOCUSED THINKER

My health caused me to move in 2018. I wanted to be closer to my sister, her family, and a few of my dear friends and just be able to take advantage of what the downtown Houston area had to offer. I stopped driving. Mostly because I was worried about the safety of everybody else on the road. I found that Jarvis, my bad leg, was really not cooperating at all. I would drive with my right hand under my right knee so I could pick my leg up if I needed to. Stupid, I know. I made the decision to start going to the theater more often since it has always been such an important part of my life. I was no longer working, so I could spend my time writing, with my fur babies and enjoying my new awesome view from the fifteenth floor.

Shortly after I moved in town, I got pneumonia, which landed me in the hospital for five weeks. Now, most people would be extremely unhappy with that. I really was not. You'll see why soon. I had to undergo some intensive physical therapy while in the hospital because I had gotten so weak.

When I was admitted into the hospital, I was using a walker—albeit not very well and for short periods of time because I would simply run out of energy. The whole time my physical therapist in the hospital said he was sending me home with the wheelchair, I mulled over it incessantly and refused. I was not happy about that. Then I was introduced to the motor on the wheelchair. This all goes back to using our brains. Damn, they're pretty savvy! I realized that the wheelchair with the motor was a way of conserving my physical energy. I could then use my walker for little things, but I use the wheelchair with the motor to go walk with my friend, Richard, and my dog, Foster, and to live. It was the smartest thing I've ever done. I go to the mall. I go to restaurants. I go to the park. I honestly never realized how important the simple act of going outside is—for sun, exercise, taking in the brilliant colors of nature, speaking to neighbors, and enjoying watching my puppy run around and have fun.

When the world was ordered to shut down, we also experienced several weeks of an African dust issue that prevented me from going outside at all. *Isolation* became a really dark word, something to loathe, but I know numerous creative professionals who turned it into an opportunity to create, pivot, expand. Inspired, I took the opportunity to start writing this book. The animals couldn't exactly participate as my co-authors, and I'm sure they got sick of me reading passages aloud to them, but those many hours spent in positivity saved me from wallowing in inertia, depression, and stagnation.

Happiness and positivity are a choice. I didn't realize how important making that choice was until being hit with the pandemic. After all, everything was already slow in my world. Living with MS can be fraught with dramatic pain and struggling to speak, breathe, swallow. I got into a dark place, as I think many people did. While talking with my friend, Mush, he asked me what I would want to say to other people who felt deep despair, isolation, and a lack of hope. As I started talking, Mush turned on his phone's video camera and helped me share a message of hope on

LinkedIn. This is how my Random Thoughts began. Just from the comments, you could tell how many people we touched. How many people had their own need to hear something positive. How connected we really are.

What I needed to hear was to take action no matter what. It is always within your power to take some kind of action that can create something good for somebody else.

If all this positivity already sounds like the daydreaming of a has-been lawyer hellbent on splashing society with his ill rants, allow me to submit the evidence that overwhelmingly supports my argument.

People with a family history of heart disease who also had a positive outlook were one-third less likely to have a heart attack or other cardiovascular event within five to twenty-five years than those with a more negative outlook. That's the finding from Johns Hopkins expert, Lisa Yanek, MPH, and her colleagues. The finding held even in people with family history who had the most risk factors for coronary artery disease, and positive people from the general population were 13 percent less likely than their negative counterparts to have a heart attack or other coronary event.

Yanek and her team determined "positive" versus "negative" outlook using a survey tool that assesses a person's cheerfulness, energy level, anxiety levels and satisfaction with health and overall life. But you don't need a survey to assess your own positivity, says Yanek. "I think people tend to know how they are." There is definitely a strong link between positivity and health. Additional studies have found that a positive attitude improves outcomes and life satisfaction across a spectrum of conditions—including traumatic brain injury, brain tumors and stroke. Conversely, negative emotions can weaken immune response.

Mindset shapes reality.

It is very difficult to stay positive when you're in a wheelchair, but I do. I don't have a choice. It's all about finding ways to adapt and taking those baby steps that are so important to live a life worth living and not just sitting around waiting to die. You have to adapt to your new life, your new normal, your new happiness.

I urge you to do things that are smart and do things that improve your quality of life. I'm extremely happy being able to go do whatever I want whenever I want to—with the chair. It presents opportunities. I cannot linger in a wishing well, wishing I did not have to look at this looming purple thing. (Yes. My wheelchair is TCU purple…of course.) I won't go anywhere wishing.

I have said that having MS was a blessing because it prevented all of the bad things happening in my life that I was certainly headed towards. Smoking. Drinking. Ignoring exercise. Living negatively. Getting pneumonia was a blessing as well since it forced me to reboot and get back into my workouts and rituals of eating healthfully and taking other actions that signify growth and goodness. We also have to intertwine negative circumstances with a positive twist. Find a way to make quarantine help you. Find a way to make illness or even great loss make you better. The bottom line is to make absolutely every challenge you face one *for* you rather than *against* you. You must make a decision that this is how you're going to live. Once again, you must choose the way you're going to live your life.

Draw in your superpower. Draw in positivity. If you need examples of how this works, I encourage you to really internalize *Nerves of Steel.* Yes, I am just another man…and with a lot of limitations. But I can assure you that my attitude helped to carve out at least twenty more precious years of beating unimaginable odds.

If you have an open mind, I open up my story to you, friend.

CHAPTER 1

HIT THE HIGH NOTES FOREVER

*"Music gives a soul to the universe, wings to the mind,
flight to the imagination and life to everything."*

—PLATO

I HAVE ALWAYS BEEN extremely active in theater and music. I was the lead in all of the plays and musicals in high school. I was the president of the choir. I continued to act in college, and I continued to sing as well. In fact, I sang in Verdi's "Requiem" as a member of the chorus with "Diva" star soprano, Wilhelmenia Fernandez and the Fort Worth Symphony Orchestra. Wilhelmenia's stunning story of cultivating her talent in Philadelphia and landing title roles in "Carmen," "Aïda," and "La Bohème" in opera houses around the world set me on fire. She came from a modest background and then was swept up in glamorous Paris to command stages with her voice. *Could that be me*, I wondered.

At this point, I spent my summers working at a Boy Scout camp eventually as the program director and directed a play at camp called "Ghost Dance." I directed a well-received play at Texas Christian University called "Young, Gifted and Black" for Black History Month, and then the "Frog Follies" pieces for the class of 1985, which was a musical dance number for an annual homecoming show.

When singing and dancing wasn't enough to satiate my musical side, I started playing handbells with an incredible handbell choir at my church. The thing about handbells is that there are various ways to play them. Many handbell ringers read off notated music, which looks a bit like piano music, as it has a treble clef and a bass clef stave; however, some ringers read from number charts, only ringing their bells when the appropriate number comes up. Just as for standard orchestral instruments, notated handbell music also contains symbols that give direction on how to play the bells in terms of damping, plucking, shaking, and many other effects. Learning and mastering all of these techniques became an obsession. So much so that eventually, I would direct the handball choirs at my church after I got married. I took them from a mediocre handbell choir that could only play three songs and three octaves of the bells to one that could play extremely difficult pieces and a full seven octaves. We would go on to play for my sister Kimi's wedding. I wrote the wedding march.

In all these roles, my lesson was hitting the highest notes of life that I possibly could. You see, "mediocrity" doesn't really exist in dynamic performance-related careers that are designed to delight audiences. At least in my mind. You don't make it to Broadway to perform in shows like "Moulin Rouge" or "Hamilton" if you're average. You don't *get by*. You don't *settle*.

Alas, at some point in all my singing, dancing and handbelling, when acting roles were presented, it dawned on me that I would be too fat and bald to be an actor. My second goal was to be a neurosurgeon, but I could not handle organic chemistry. At the same time, my hands actually tremored in college, which was another reason why I didn't think I could perform surgeries. I was told that my busy hands tremored because I drank too much coffee or was too high-strung. Looking back, this was most likely early signs of MS. I switched to political science with an eye on becoming a lawyer.

I attended South Texas College of Law and accentuated my law school days by traveling with a superior mock trial team. Mock trials are a powerful way to test your ability to argue a case, explain legal basis and facts, present exhibits, cross-examine on the absence of evidence, serve as a witness, and write briefs. Our mighty team won many tournaments including the 1988 Thelen, Marrin, Johnson & Bridges Mock Trial Competition and the State Moot Court Championship, and I will always be proud of those accolades.

I became a medical malpractice trial lawyer, which perfectly suited my theatrical impulses. I demonstrated my acting in front of my audience (the jury) and I got my dose of "practicing medicine" because I was representing doctors. I was fortunate enough to have the kind of relationship with my clients to scrub in for surgery. After all, how can you explain what happens in a complicated back surgery where they are using tools that look like they came out of the garage, if you have not seen it? I really dug into the acting part of my role. I remember a particular closing argument in which the plaintiffs did not have a theory of where a blood clot formed. One theory was that it came from the brain. One theory was that it came from the spine. I told the jury that the plaintiffs were so desperate to come up with a theory that one was that "*Shazam*, it was just there!" See, there was theatre involved in all these narratives for sure. I proudly served as a trial attorney for twenty-five years.

If we all strived to hit the high note in everything we do, can you imagine our collective performance?

For me these days, the task can be as simple as how many times and how high I lift a leg with my physical therapist. The feeling of knowing I gave it my all is exhilarating and lifts me into the next task fluidly, whereas, if my gut tells me I'm not trying and just want to get it over with so I can binge more Netflix, the feeling is mild irritation that can build and throw me into sadness or even anger. Then that is what I carry throughout my day, resulting in more stress in my body. I can't afford not to hit the high notes.

CHAPTER 2

LISTEN TO YOUR TRUSTED TRIBE

"Take care of your body. It's the only place you have to live."

—Jim Rohn

MET MY TRUE love, Shannon, on a blind date. We had a lengthy lunch that easily turned into dinner. We got engaged a week later and married a year after that. She did not want to wait until after I took the bar exam to get married, so we had a huge society wedding two days after I graduated from law school and on a Tuesday, a few days before Christmas. Needless to say, it wasn't the ideal time to host a big Texan wedding, but love inspires a lot of crazy shenanigans, and so do endlessly supportive parents who love a great party and teach their kids that everything is possible.

If you were to interview all three kids, we would give you a different characterization of my dad. But out of all of the versions of my dad, we all agreed that he was the epitome of Texas—grit and making the most of yourself as an individual. You own your actions, decisions, emotions, and outcomes, and where you came from a minute ago or even at birth does not dictate where you are going.

My dad had been adopted. His biological mother had an alcoholic husband, and my dad was the oldest and would go stay with his aunt and uncle in Fort Worth during various times in his early life. They lost twin boys, barely two years old, to the Spanish flu, and offered to take care of "Richard" and adopted him as a toddler and he went from an "Adams" to a "Sherer" for his last name. Grandma and Grandpa Sherer were the only paternal grandparents we knew and boy, did they love us and us, them. In middle school, we learned the story of my dad's adoption. We also got lucky to meet our biological paternal grandmother, and she was in our life from that point on.

Friends have heard me say, "Can't never did nothing."

It's Texan slang for, "Figure it out! You can do everything in life," which my dad would always state. To him, everything was possible. The word "can't" wasn't in his vocabulary. This was a powerful driver for us as kids to think, *oh, I can do whatever I am capable of.* Our brother, Randy, possessed demons and difficulties finding his own happiness and drive to find a path forward. He was the sweetest and kindest of all of us—he just struggled with finding motivation and his purpose each day. Add in decades of drug use, and any motivation he might have had would never be actualized. This put a lot of pressure on our family. It was a happy, fun home, but everyone had to pitch in. We got things done as a family and everyone had to create their own path forward. There were expectations. For example, as young men, Randy and I were raised to respect women in every way, that no gender was better than the other. We were brought up to know that our sister could do anything she put her mind to, and she was a woman who should be respected, thanks to the example our dad set with both her and our mom. I do not see gender or race for the matter; I see human beings. That is just how we were raised, fortunately.

Dad was also irreverent and comedic. Correction: He was the cover guy for worst jokes ever! He was loving and loud. It hurt harder to disappoint him between the two, but he and Mom were the parents you wanted to please because of the expectations of the family. He was an entrepreneur and inventor with dozens of patents. He was a dreamer who executed on every dream. My mom worked alongside him and they achieved a lot of monumental feats over the course of their forty-three-year marriage. He had tall shoes to fill as a doctoral candidate at UCLA. During the Second World War, he was a RM3/c with the United States Coast Guard and served in both the European and Pacific Theaters and was a 2nd Lt., Cav. with the 49th Armored Division of the Texas National Guard. He was also a 32nd degree Mason.

The year 1989 is often described as a turning point in political history as the fall of the Berlin Wall triggered the collapse of the Soviet Union, but there was also a huge impact on the energy industry after the Exxon Valdez oil spill. The disaster happened when an Exxon Shipping Co. oil tanker crashed into the Prince William Sound Bligh Reef, just off the coast of Alaska, and spilled almost 11 million gallons of crude oil. The disaster led to the passage of the Oil Pollution Act 1990, which increased penalties for companies that spill oil into oceans and rivers.

Amidst this turning point was my dad's invention, a heat exchange tube insertion tool. Not a glamorous name whatsoever, but this is a piece of equipment allowing real-time repairs at the actual rigs. If a rig in the ocean went down, you would have the expense in time and trouble to bring the rig in and fix the rig. He invented the ability to go ahead and repair it while still being out at the rig, cutting down tremendous time and cost.

Dad took this invention to market and almost immediately, the patent was infringed on—the patent was stolen by a company out of Oregon in order for approximately $38 million of equipment to be produced for a division of the U.S. Armed Forces. My parents filed a lawsuit, won about $16 million, and then it lost on appeal because of sloppy attorney work.

Naturally, my parents were stressed to the bone, watching a lifetime of their efforts together going down the toilet. My dad didn't stop during a time of distress and discouragement though. In oil and gas and manufacturing, he was always thinking of how to make something better. His career provided to us three kids every opportunity to do what we wanted to do. In turn, all three of us helped him at work and worked in the factory during summers and on vacation. We would work trade shows in Mexico as product demonstrators. No surprise, I treated the product demonstrations like animated mini-shows for Randy and Kimi's amusement.

My dad was very conscientious about alcoholism because of the genetic seed of addiction, which exacerbated the situation with my brother, Randy. Randy's substance abuse problems continuously pulled at our parents and caused constant stress, drama, sadness, anger, and frustration. It inadvertently placed me and Kimi into a position of sharing some of the pain, which strengthened our bond. While I was a senior in high school, she was a freshman. I drove her to school, and she followed me into many a theatre to perform when she wasn't busy socializing like the beautiful butterfly she is to this day.

Looking back, we grew up in a cheesy picture of childhood; we lived in a safe neighborhood and walked around barefoot and went on crazy adventures. I think back on those times when the three of us put on makeshift concerts, with Randy playing guitar and Kimi playing piano. Randy is no longer with us. Kimi? As of this writing, she is working on a Ph.D. in international business involving things like EI (emotional intelligence) compared to AI (artificial intelligence), human brain and how we learn, business ethics, new workforce dynamics and current economic factors, and entrepreneurship. At the height of the coronavirus, she finalized mapping her Ph.D. program roadmap and started her second company after successfully selling her first one.

Without a doubt, I'm the quintessential proud big brother, but our bond is rare for siblings our age, I believe, and it goes beyond patting each other on the back for milestones. I trust her blindly.

Kimi was the first person to recognize that something was profoundly wrong with me. She saw me tremoring. She witnessed me running into walls and squinting through blurred vision. Slurring my words. I confided in her about urinary issues right before I collapsed on my thirty-sixth birthday, breaking a solid wooden chair right in front of her and my wife. Kimi urged me to stop everything and go for every test conceivable.

Even after this embarrassing and frightening incident, I protested a little. …Okay, *a lot*. I was supposed to start legal defense in a huge trial, representing a team of esteemed doctors. But Kimi insisted that I prioritize my health. I couldn't even say that my dramatic fall was due to a nice colorful birthday drinkie. Kimi knew I hadn't been drinking. She knew me and realized something was up. She wasn't going to stop until we figured it out.

If Kimi hadn't used tough love to pry me out of my stubbornness, she would be the one writing my story, with me six feet under (and talking about being Mom's favorite even though I vehemently disagree). Trust your tribe, let them help you. Sometimes they have a better sense of what you need than you do. And if you don't claim to have a tribe, find one. It doesn't have to be a polished group with a slew of common interests, traits and experiences. It can be one person who simply connects with you, gets you, has your back, and shows that they care about your wellbeing. They're present for the fall and the celebration. For some people, it's who they call at 3:00 a.m. from jail, but Kimi might kill me if I do!

CHAPTER 3

PROCESS AN UNSETTLING CONFIRMATION

"I say I am stronger than fear."

—Malala Yousafzai

THE PROCESS OF obtaining a diagnosis for a complex disease like MS can be funny business. I had been misdiagnosed for *years*. Recommendations were flimsy. "Cut off coffee." "You need glasses." "You're impotent." "Stop drinking." Every single symptom was missed because doctors and specialists treated it like an isolated incident.

Doctors diagnose multiple sclerosis (MS) by eliminating other conditions. They may perform a neurological exam to determine any loss of function in the nervous system, abnormal nerve reflexes, or decreased or abnormal sensations. Patients suffering from decreases in function of two different parts of the nervous system may have MS. The physician may also conduct an eye exam or a lumbar puncture. What's happening is that MS disrupts communication between the brain and other parts of the body. Thus, MS can affect the nerve cells in any part of the brain or spinal cord. Symptoms run amok.

Those suffering from MS may experience any of the following symptoms that differ greatly from person to person. Over the course of the disease and depending on the location of affected nerve fibers, the disease may manifest as:

- Numbness or weakness in one or more limbs that typically occurs on one side of your body at a time, or your legs and trunk
- Electric-shock sensations that occur with certain neck movements, especially bending the neck forward (or what is known in the medical world as Lhermitte's sign)
- Tremor, lack of coordination or unsteady gait

- Vision problems are also common, including:
- Partial or complete loss of vision, usually in one eye at a time, often with pain during eye movement
- Prolonged double vision
- Blurry vision
- Slurred speech
- Fatigue
- Dizziness
- Tingling or pain in parts of your body
- Problems with sexual, bowel and bladder function

Those suffering from MS endure attacks lasting anywhere from a couple of days to several months. These episodes vary in length and severity. Following an attack is a period of reduced or no symptoms called a *remission*. The disease often returns, or relapses, however, and the disease may continue to worsen overtime. I should point out that I have been diagnosed with primary-progressive MS in which it is very rare to have any remissions and relapses, and symptoms gradually worsen from the onset.

Knowing all this info, you can see why there was sheer confusion about what I was experiencing.

By the time I ended up in the hospital after my thirty-sixth birthday, "Texas Super Doc" Dr. Igor Churches of The Neurology Center connected the dots. I knew of his specialties in headaches, balance disorders, neuromuscular disorders, low back pain, and neck pain. It was as if I was this doctor's vivid poster child for all of these ailments. This smorgasbord of aches and pains had been my entire adult life.

Lynn Maki, nurse manager at The Neurology Center and affectionately known in the office as the future ex-Mrs. Sherer, describes the disease's progression since we met. I am deliberately keeping the integrity of her words to capture the warning signs and magnitude of this disease in case it can help someone else: "He was walking and relatively stable. He had weakness on one side, but he was still walking without any assist device. Some of the more obvious symptoms to get your primary care doctors thinking are visual, information of the optic nerve that would be a red flag, along with numbness or tingling in an extremity, one hand or one leg, and the person doesn't have any underlying condition that would justify. Maybe they are not diabetic or with a back injury, but they have the numbness or tingling—something that would trigger needing an MRI. Then suspicion of MS. Your typical presentation, if not optic neuritis, would be numbness in an extremity. Trace would have his one leg dragging or numb. He would walk and his stance was a little off, legs further apart to maintain balance. But he was still working fulltime. In people with stressful careers, you see the diagnosis of autoimmune disease come up more frequently due to *stress*. And it's a big trigger for MS. Trace had a stressful job. But he wanted to get on treatment quickly and tried to prevent progression of the disease.

"He has always been very medication compliant, but compared to where he was when we met to now, he doesn't walk today. A lot of patients at the beginning can miss a shot because they never had to do injections themselves at home and the cause is travel or work. But Trace was pretty compliant. He likes to say he is the 'perfect patient'! Despite compliance, his disease progressed. We had to go with bigger medications to help control his disease. MS in and of itself is a progressive disease, with more types of physical disability showing up, even with treatment. It is a debilitating disease. There were four or five medicines before. Now, there are nineteen different medications, along with more studies to try to stop disability, but it is very individual. There are like 200,000 cases a year. In the general population, the prevalence was 309 per 100,000 people. It is more aggressive with Trace because it affects his mobility and speech. The medicine is only as good as it is for 'you' because it's different for every 'body'."

As I experienced the assaults on my body, the "what" of MS, I used to be desperate to find the cause. The condition generally develops between the ages of twenty and forty, but how?

In medical terms, courtesy of The Neurology Center: "A myelin sheath is a protective covering surrounding nerve cells. When these are damaged, nerve signals slow down or stop altogether, causing multiple sclerosis. It is unknown what causes the myelin sheath to deteriorate or become damaged, but it may be linked to genetics, certain viruses, or environmental factors."

When it comes to illness, "unknown" is a brutally frustrating word. It needles you. It can eat you alive if you focus on it. I would never receive a definitive answer on why this disease pulverized my body. I also realized that "reasons" are empty promises. I may have been able to prevent MS from finding me if I had a less stressful and busy life. Helping my wife navigate her own struggles with bipolar depression certainly added to my pressures. But she had a mental affliction, and I strived to add value to her life journey—even if just a little. None of this information or musings about an alternate life would serve my health.

What I *could* do is commit to medications to slow the progression, medications to ease the symptoms, physical therapy, assistive devices (hearing aids, wheelchairs, bed lifts, etc.), and behavioral and dietary changes. This was straight from the doctor's mouth when I inquired about treatment with a feigned blank face. *Okay, I can take these steps*, I thought. Inside, I crackled with emotion, calculating the past decade of my life, which now seemed to go by so rapidly. In 1988, I got married and became a lawyer; 1990, became a father to my first son; 1992, had my second son; and 1999, encountered a debilitating disease I now had a label for, yet absolutely no end date for other than death. When would it kill me?

…*Wait a minute. Hold up.*

I was giving away my power, my legacy just like that? The singer-dancer-lawyer in me couldn't go down without a show—the most epic show of strength, resilience, grit, grace. I took a lot of time to emotionally process this new reality. I'm not sure that illness is something to "get used to" exactly, particularly a disease that holds wicked surprises, inflicting small and big attacks on your body like a thief in the night, but you can learn to live with limitations. These limitations can present new ways of thinking like a sleuth and discovering untapped methods and possibilities. I had to operate from this mindset.

Mindset is a *choice*. I could choose to be positive despite pain, despite setbacks, and even giving up my career as an attorney, which would perhaps be the most bitter pill to swallow.

Even though I was already set on fighting MS, Shannon's father, a radiologist, insisted that I obtain a second opinion. The second-opinion doctor said that I would likely be in a wheelchair by the end of the year and dead by 2001. In the calendar year of 2021, I am here to tell you that there was no chance in hell I would accept this! At the same time, I knew that Dr. Cherches would never have given me an opinion like this and would in fact, find it obscenely irresponsible. He and Lynn have been amazing in how they have handled me and my treatment.

CHAPTER 4

BREAK THROUGH, DON'T BREAK DOWN

"If you are lucky enough to never experience any sort of adversity, we won't know how resilient you are. It's only when you're faced with obstacles, stress, and other environmental threats that resilience, or the lack of it, emerges: Do you succumb, or do you surmount?"

—MARIA KONNIKOVA

RECENTLY LEARNED ABOUT Joe Dimeo, who underwent the world's first successful face and hands transplant after 80 percent of his body was burned in a car accident. The whopping 140 health care pros it took to complete the twenty-three-hour procedure were obviously amazing, but based on everything I read about Dimeo's condition, so was his attitude. He had already endured twenty reconstructive surgeries, and he kept his spirits high—even as he was told that he could die from this extremely rare procedure. It had only been attempted twice in the world, with both attempts failing and sadly, one of the patients dying.

Dimeo said, "You can always look on the downside of things, but there's always more good things than bad things."

Based on my own experience, I'll wager that Dimeo's positive outlook is paramount to his very existence. This doesn't mean that there isn't intense suffering or struggles. Positivity doesn't cancel pain. It operates concurrently with it, and sometimes, yes, positivity supersedes pain or makes it more bearable at a minimum. Positivity emits energy, and raises vibration inwardly and outwardly.

When I informed my sons about my diagnosis, it was excruciating. They knew me as a go-getter, a white-collar professional who could provide what they needed and wanted, a father who was involved in the community, in the church, and leading hikes in Estes Park. My career allowed them to have a stay-at-home mom, which she had always wanted to be and was really good at it. She played sports with them, hitting pop flies and grounders into their oversized gloves. We, as parents, never missed a game, and to do so would have been out of the question for Shannon. With her constant encouragement in particular, Preston played competitive baseball as a six-year-old. I'm not talking about the Little League; way beyond. Real tournaments for that age.

Heat exposure can cause or heighten fatigue, numbness, blurry vision, tremor, confusion, imbalance, and weakness, so I was repeatedly scolded for going to my boys' games. What else could I do but be there to watch them hit line drives? I could no longer lead them on hikes up mountains or treks through the woods. I could be their biggest cheerleader though. I had to be *there* for my sons however I possibly could.

Everyone calls me stubborn, but if I were not "stubborn," I can guarantee you that I wouldn't be alive. My son, Trevor, will tell you the same. He tells his friends I'm at least ten years past my "expiration date"!

Unfortunately, I was increasingly sick at a pivotal age in my sons' lives. I have faith that they've seen the way that I've tried to exemplify a positive role model over the years, despite deterioration on the outside.

My kids also had to endure the sudden separation of their parents. Our marriage couldn't withstand the pressure. We took vows for times of "sickness and health," but we became one of the couples in the high divorce rate of married couples due to a spouse becoming ill.

I vividly remember an occasion when Shannon came to my apartment after the divorce and said, "I just don't understand why you can always be so happy and positive." I told her that was the only way I could live and deal with my disease. She eventually started living life this way and she was elated to see the change this attitude brought her.

After we got divorced, Shannon needed to get her own health insurance based on the mandates from insurance companies and how long an ex-spouse is allowed to stay on the primary insurer's policy. She did not before she with diagnosed breast cancer and subsequently, moved into my house. Two sick divorcees living together when we could have just stayed married. I know it sounds uncanny and bizarre. Nevertheless, as a colorful showcase of positivity, instead of making room for a sickness den as Shannon underwent chemo, we had her room done in fabrics and paints that she would enjoy.

As an epilogue here, we vacationed together, and when Shannon got remarried, we continued to be close. Our friendship developed in a different way than it could have in the rigors of marriage and co-illnesses. Her husband became a friend, and we would spend the holidays together with the family and all of the kids. We really had a very positive divorce! I guess this is the "Trace" way and it became the Shannon way.

For the purpose of this book, I talked to my son, Trevor, about his recollection of being raised by two ill parents. He shared some profound things I never knew. I also consider his viewpoint an important window into a mature adult whose childhood was severely disrupted. "I don't consider that either of you raised me, though you instilled some great things. I'm lucky in terms of growing up quickly and accepting that life isn't always easy. A couple of years after both of you got sick, I would stay awake at night thinking about heaven and hell, both places being equally frightening because they are 'forever'. This is probably why I am agnostic. The idea that you're going somewhere forever freaks me out."

He also pointed out that his brother, Preston, had to deal with everything at an even younger age. Preston also has bipolar disorder, which wore on Trevor. Shannon didn't start taking medicine for bipolar depression until her last couple of years, which is unfortunate because it truly helped her in so many ways.

Trevor adds: "On my twenty-fifth birthday, Mom got put on hospice. I kick myself because that day, I played golf with friends. I put off what was really going on though I was there when she passed away. My life has been lived to not have my mom worry. Then you just want me to be happy. You have given me unconditional love. I am forever grateful for that."

In this bizarre set of circumstances that had been dealt to my sons, I always strived to be an open person and a great communicator. They knew they could always talk to me. This prompted them to tell their friends to confide in me if they needed a trusted adult to talk to. If any of the friends are in town, they make it a point to see me. I listen to whatever is on their mind.

The man that Shannon married is an extremely bright Green Beret. I know he taught my sons perhaps what I would have taught them if my body had stayed intact. Then again, I was a Boy Scout, not a Green Beret! No competition. He was good to them and for them, wonderful to Shannon, and he included me in activities, which he didn't have to but chose to.

Shannon was the only person I've ever truly loved and

was my best friend until she passed away. In fact, the day she died, I held her hand and sat with her for some time. I paused. I paused to honor her life. I paused to recognize, really see, all that her life represented.

Leading up to her death, I considered her to be more peaceful and positive than I had ever known her to be. She broke through in her last stage of life rather than breaking down, even though her long history foretold breaking down inside a nest of misery until the very end. In her final hours, she radiated a gorgeous glow.

This message of breaking through, not breaking down, has a lot of resonance. I recently shared one of my signature Random Thoughts short videos, which goes as follows: "I have a physical therapist that comes twice a week. We start and end each session with a timed stand. Usually at the end, the timed stand is worthless since I'm very tired and have exhausted myself already. In addition, I didn't have an appetite for several months, so I was very concerned. In the past few weeks, my timed stand is doubling and even tripling. And I'm ravenous. I'm ravenous for good food. I want fruits and vegetables. The other day, I craved a wedge salad. Who craves a wedge salad? I asked my physical therapist, 'Why are we seeing all these improvements very suddenly?' He looked at me and smiled. He said, 'It's because you're happy.' Holy cow! I'm improving my medical condition because I'm happy. Besides wanting to scream to all of you to start that journey since I have a writing project that is so close to being finished [yep, this book!], I want to finish it. Start your journey. But I also want you to think, what happens if every single one of us makes ourselves better by becoming happier? Think of the power of positivity, joy and happiness we as a society create. Every journey starts with one step. Take one strong, safe step today. Tomorrow, take two."

My memories of my brother, Randy, begin when he started high school. We moved to Texas from Illinois, and the transition was arduous for him. He was a hockey player moving to the South, a hot spot for baseball and basketball for boys his age. I don't think he ever felt that he belonged. Randy started hanging out with a crowd that did drugs early on. He was not present. As I got older, I realized it was because he was high. My mind flashes to Alice Cooper posters, with the smell of weed trailing him everywhere. My parents didn't know what to do, so they tried tough love and pushed him to work for their office. He was gifted and proved to be a phenomenal draftsman, but he didn't want to do anything. He didn't even want to get out of bed after being up all night.

Kimi and I don't have a lot of memories that were not wrapped around him being under the influence or causing my parents drama. At least his excess served to turn us off from trying recreational drugs. We saw the devastation that can do for a family.

Kimi had broken ties for our entire family from Randy years before his death because of the havoc his addiction was causing my mom and me. Randy used Kimi as an endless money pit. She was the one trying to convince him to get into therapy and rehab. She was also protecting a sick brother and a sick mom to not feel the pain and hurt of being around an addict. To tell you the truth, I was so ill during the week that he died, the sequence of events is blurry. That said, this blurriness did not take away from the magnitude of this tragedy for me when it happened. If anything, it exacerbated the feeling of helplessness.

Helplessness is a horrible place to be in. It doesn't lend an opening for breaking through. Helplessness is often the last stop before breaking down.

As I was trying to put the pieces together of Randy's life, Kimi informed me: "When I saw him a few years before his death, I thought, *he's on meth*. The teeth, the face. I had just known someone we did an intervention for. He was calling you, telling you that helicopters were overhead, and the police were coming to get him. He would call you because he knew you would be nicer and that I would no longer be convinced of his stories or come to his rescue anymore. He needed to get help and be ready for it. He was a danger to my kids. He was a danger to you and Mom. I was constantly trying to do personal intervention, so we had to extract from him. I knew until he helped himself, this would continuously be a painful cycle of hurt, worry, heartbreak, and deception for all of us."

Our brother didn't go quietly in the wind. He did a great deal of damage years leading up to his death. Some events, pretty striking. But those who have encountered a loved one's rocky road of addiction can relate to just how bad it gets. For example, after my dad had been gone for ten years, my mom finally decided to sell his collection of guns. Kimi kept insisting that we sell the guns for money for Mom, but she didn't want to part with them at first. Then we were connected to a Federal Firearms Licensed

(FFL) dealer, Ken, through a friend. Kimi took one of her best friend's sons, Ross, to help with the moving around of the guns out to Mom's house to meet Ken to go through the inventory. Our brilliant dad had built their house with all these sneaky places behind the walls to store guns, like behind the air conditioner vent! He was a genius.

Mom had listed the complete inventory of the guns and had done her research on the valuation, which had amounted to approximately $250,000. Mom didn't care about the value and we were uncomfortable about the guns being in the house, so the best situation was Ken's interest in the complete list and commitment to buying the collection that day.

According to Kimi, Mom sat down with her long list of itemized guns, serial numbers, dates, cost of purchase, and estimated value. She directed Ross where to start pulling out guns from various hideaways in the home.

When Ross made his way to a box, Mom instructed, "Be careful. It's heavy!"

He handled it effortlessly and she said, "You are so strong."

Ross said, "This is really light. Is there anything in here?"

Kimi picks up the dramatic story here. It's a prime example of our mother's upstanding character. "I stopped. My heart sank. He opened the box, and it was empty. My face probably turned white. Mom said, 'That's interesting. Go ahead and get the other box.' She was super positive, but I knew. He pulled out the next box. *Empty.* Third box, her face turned grey. I'll never forget the color. Grey. I remember thinking, *wow*. She sat there and looked at me. I went down to the other part of the house where she could not hear. I called Randy and I wanted to ensure that I didn't sound accusatory, but I knew he was the only one who knew where every single gun was stored in the home. It went to voicemail. I said, 'I'm at Mom's and we have a federal firearms licensed dealer. You are the only one who knows where these guns are, so we would love your help in guiding us on how to find them. Can you call me back? I wanted to say, 'You damned well know where these guns are! You better call back!' I went back and a dozen boxes were empty. My mom could not speak. She had more grace than anyone you will meet. I said, 'I'm on it.' She said, 'I can't believe this. I'm hoping there is an explanation.' I told Ken, 'My brother, Randy, is the only one who knows where these guns are. And he's also a drug addict. And he's also caused a lot of stress on this family.' Ken, a complete stranger, got up and walked over to my mom and touched her hand, saying, 'My son fought addiction his whole life until he got clean eighteen months ago. He stopped and helped someone who had a flat tire and got killed by an eighteen-wheeler. I know the pain that you are going through and I am here.' A complete stranger was put in our lives for a specific reason that day. And clearly, it wasn't to buy my dad's gun collection, but rather, to be there as a someone who had firsthand knowledge of dealing with a child with addiction.

"I kept calling Randy until he picked up the phone. He was crying, screaming that he owed people money and they threatened to kill Mom and you…that they didn't know my married last name or would come and find me, too. I told Randy, you have twenty-four hours to figure out how to get this fixed or we call the police.' Hung up. I knew those guns were gone since she was in the hospital earlier that year, so there was an opportunity to go into the house and get them. I also knew they were gone by the sound of his voice. We never heard another word about the guns."

A decision was made that day by our mom who, after a few hours, said directly to Kimi that she wouldn't press charges, but she wanted to completely sever ties with him. She felt that this was the last straw of deception and unless he would get help and get clean, this was a danger to our entire family both physically and emotionally.

Ironically, the gun Randy eventually used to shoot himself was registered under his name. It wasn't part of my dad's collection. This haunts me, alongside his death. Where are those guns now? What mayhem have they caused?

One morning in mid-February, I got a call from the police and then I called Kimi, who was leading a client's leadership offsite workshop for three days with 150 people. She has a good friend in the police department who she requested welfare checks from in the past on Randy just to ensure he was okay regardless of her having no direct contact with him. He would keep her informed of where Randy was living and how he was doing. She called him.

"At first, I thought it was a scam because Randy would say outrageous stories to try and get money from us," Kimi adds. "My police officer friend texted me three minutes later to tell me Randy was on his way to the hospital—that he was not allowed to tell me as official business, but Randy tried to take his own life. At first, I thought it was a cry for help…again. I ended up leaving the meeting and one of my best friends covered for me in the rest of the meeting. I went to the hospital and you were already there. Basically, the doctor said he would not survive. He shot himself in the mouth and it went through his brain, but he still had brain activity. It was a matter of when the brain died. We knew if there was good to come out of such tragedy, it would be the donation of his organs. So the doctors kept him on life support to keep his organs healthy while his body decided on its own terms when his exit on earth would be. We're going to keep him on life support until his body shut down. We're all organ donors."

I do remember talking to the doctor.

Kimi said, "I want to see Randy."

I said no, trying to muster some big-brother authority, but she needed it for closure. I said, "If you're going, I am." We went in together and said our goodbye. It made me cry. His death wasn't unexpected, but it was still tragic. How can someone hurt so much that they can't muster anything else, that they can't get help or go to a shelter? At least he was in peace after so much turmoil. Randy was fifty-six years old. He actually lived longer than we expected.

Here, I want to point out how our lives all intersected with this tragedy. Even in the gravity of losing her other brother, taking care of our mother, and taking care of her business, Kimi, as my trusted tribe, took care of me. She knows what stress does to my body. It's like putting a match to a candle.

On the Tuesday that Randy shot himself, he was still alive…clinically. Kimi had to answer the doctor's questions related to him being an organ donor. Did he shoot heroin? Smoke weed? Snort cocaine?

Kimi said, "My brother is an addict. We cut ties with him about five years ago. I don't know *all* he has done or been addicted to. I don't know about his lifestyle. I don't know if he was straight or gay. I don't know about his overall health anymore."

They said, "It won't interfere. We just need to understand someone's background as you can remember." They explained they have a very rigorous process to test all organs to determine what is or is not viable.

On Wednesday, with no change in Randy's condition, Kimi went back to work her client. She called several times throughout the day to check on his status. Nothing in Randy's condition had changed. You're literally *waiting* for the body to die. Well, my birthday was that Thursday. Kimi told the doctor, "You cannot let him die tomorrow because that is my other brother, Trace's birthday." The doctor was so amazing. She said, "We won't let that happen." Thursday night, no change.

On Friday, Kimi wanted to go to Randy's apartment. Her husband, Michael, and one of our best friends, Mush, tried to discourage her from it, but instead, they escorted her so she wouldn't have to go through the surreal experience alone. Randy had been the one to call 9-1-1 himself. He thought he would be successful in his suicide. Kimi wanted to see his space and try and understand his state of mind. Upon entrance, everything was so organized. He left notes and various things in stacks for each of us. He went through his trash to see if he was using drugs at the time and just grasping at a "reason." In his trash was a wadded-up note, a list of final things to do. "Do the laundry, fold it, put the note out for Kimi and Trace, take the cat to boarding." One of last items noted was "say prayers," and he was not a religious man. This walk-through of his apartment was an important step for Kimi and her healing process. The doctor could not believe Randy was still alive on Friday.

Saturday morning, he passed away. This began the process of organ donation, which would give us a powerful and positive path forward coming from such darkness and tragedy. For months, we were worried Mom would have regrets, but she felt she had tried to help him for decades and did everything she could. She said she would always feel sadness that a human would feel this much despair to not get help that was continuously offered, but she knew we all did what we could. This was a supreme breakthrough for a mother who lost her child to suicide.

One of the most important things I've learned in my amazing journey of life is that through every tragedy, there usually is some goodness. Randy's organs have helped many people, but we have a very special bond with a gentleman that received Randy's kidney. We have enjoyed spending time with him, and he and his family even spent a Christmas with us.

CHAPTER 5

OPTIMISM IS A TOOL

"So, the darkness shall be the light,
and the stillness the dancing."

—*T.S. Elliott*

Y MOM ALWAYS had a positive outlook, even when we irritated her as kids. She would turn the music up and whistle. She was an optimist through the litany of stuff she has been through in the categories of health, family, and business. Mom kept going because of her inner spirit. I have it, too, and so does my sister. I'm grateful she taught me grit, that there will always be a solution.

While Mom had the lightness, my dad became bitter with the legal battle over their business. It took him away emotionally for the last two years of his life. His health declined so fast. Did he create that energy? Mom still tried to be the happy, positive, strong one. At the age of 70, my mom had to realize how to take care of herself. She had to practice her own stories, her own belief systems.

Before she passed away at the age of 89, while I was writing this book, in fact, my mom's body was like a 140-year-old and her spirit continued to dance and frolic like a 35-year-old woman. At her peak weight, she weighed 350 pounds. She put a lot of wear and tear on her body, smoking two or more packs of cigarettes a day, lying out in the sun with baby oil, and carrying a lot of stress from my parents' company that did really well until the oil crash in the 1980s. My dad's best friend, an attorney, was stealing from him. We won a large settlement, newsworthy at the time, and by the time my parents found out about the theft, they were almost bankrupt. It put so much stress on them. My mom was taking care of her mom, as well as my dad until he died. In essence, she gained a lot of weight from emotional eating. After my father passed away, she started losing weight on her own. She lost approximately seventy pounds and reached a plateau.

She didn't have many friends left after taking care of everyone else and not cultivating friendships. She joined Weight Watchers, which changed her life. She gained many great friends and lost weight. Her body deteriorated though with open heart surgery, melanoma, organs removed. My goodness, she was like a bionic woman! Kept coming back from serious health conditions for more life and positive moments, as the power of her spirit kept her obliterated body alive.

A few months before she died, I had the pleasure of asking my mother if she would do anything differently. She paused thoughtfully and then said that she didn't have any regrets, only lessons for doing things differently next time. I see this grace and kindness in my sister's children, too. They elevate the experience of life for anyone in their orbit. Things translate to something good, positive impact.

My mom and I had decided a long time ago that when we wake up and look in the mirror, we want to think about the good things coming, not bad things. She wired my sister and me like this, and Kimi handed this down to her children, Emerson and Mac. When Randy had taken his life, he was not one that looked for the good things in life. We learned a lesson from that. The three of us were the highlight of my mother's life. In her honor, Kimi and I will carry on the family story of countless happy endings, even if small or subtle.

Because isn't that the real story? How you come through. It has helped all of us survive. Life is pretty hard sometimes. It is a battle. It is purposeful to say we're born to do hard things, but this is the lifecycle to get to the good.

I've been asked, if you are not naturally positive, how

do you change that wiring? In a book that tells this story, will it connect to people who are not wired for positivity and not being the victim anymore and owning the good side of life, not the dark? What can people do on their own?

Let me tell you, I have shitty moments every day of my life. In quarantine, for example, before I started writing, I felt down, defeated, and bored. My mom had been locked up and going out of her mind, too. We were two sick, comical crazies in quarantine! Sometimes, several body parts are simply throbbing in intense pain, trying to see which one screams louder. At times, I'm frustrated I cannot work and contribute to a greater good. Please pay attention here. The way I choose to come out of the mindset of being down is critical. MS is debilitating, but it's about how I return to that battle every day. I am literally fighting the negative with my amazing spirit, infused with the grit that both of my parents handed down. You have an amazing spirit. We all do.

I wouldn't call any days "good" in the way of my physical body in perhaps five or six years. I've fallen on the floor without calling anyone. By the time I got up by myself, the century had turned. Just kidding! I admit, I would stay on the floor all night. My mom exhibited this behavior. Kimi used to joke, "You decided to have a sleepover on the floor?", flabbergasted we didn't call her. Lesson: Grit can work against us sometimes. Neither of us wanted to die on the floor in the name of grit or bravado. We simply didn't want to put anyone else out.

There may not be great days of parade and confetti, but there may be a celebration for the way you go into the battle. You can't go in with a cynical attitude. Mom was bound and determined to drive again. A shiny new car rested in the driveaway. Well, it became reckless for her to drive again! She didn't get to sit behind the steering wheel. She held onto that dream of driving again until her last days.

What is good in the world in this hour? Focus on that. If that doesn't work to change how you feel, try to go a little deeper and gauge if you can do one of the following:

1. Practice gratitude. List what you are grateful for. I know a lot of people who keep gratitude journals and write in them first thing in the morning or as the last activity before sleeping.

2. Do something nice for someone. It can be anything from sending flowers "just because" to picking up the phone and just listening to the details of their day.

3. Stop the negative self-talk. You produce your own positive energy by laughing and talking to yourself with compassion, the way that you would speak to a loved one.

4. Celebrate everything. Celebration is the elixir of life.

5. Surround yourself with positive people. During the quarantine at the height of the coronavirus, you saw musicians playing instruments and singing on balconies across the globe, and life coaches and fitness trainers on video pumping up the masses. Even if you were alone in your apartment yet witnessed some of this, you were surrounding yourself with positive people.

CHAPTER 6

REINVENT, OR RETHINK MOTION

"You can't move mountains by whispering at them."

—*PINK*

THE WORD "ATHLETE" and Trace Sherer never appeared in the same thought or sentence. But as I felt more and more physically bad, and things were out of control inside my body, I sought ways to test my endurance. I wasn't the only one in the world grappling with these limitations and choices.

Michelle Tolson, a dance teacher of over thirty years and a former Radio City Rockette, faced the diagnosis of MS, which could leave her disabled. She wondered if she would have to quit teaching, if she would end up in a wheelchair, and who would take care of her.

She stated for the National MS Society: "I can't stress this enough. When diagnosed, I was told that I had probably had the disease for over ten years, but because I had been so active, I never noticed symptoms. Get out and take a walk. Get some light hand weights and exercise at home while you are watching TV. Stretch, if you can, every day. The more you do for your body, the better your body will treat you. It is a sneaky disease that leaves you feeling different each and every day. Some days you will totally feel like yourself. Some days you will feel like you need to sleep for 24 hours. Reading shared information, joining groups, and volunteering my time with others that understand what I am going through makes me feel 'normal' again. I will be celebrating seven years of living with MS in March of 2021. Yes, I use the word 'celebrating' because I still teach, I still dance, I still mentor, I still volunteer."

Reality TV star Jack Osbourne learned he has multiple sclerosis in 2012. He told the British magazine *Hello* that "'adapt and overcome' is my new motto." Just two months later, he took to Twitter to tell the world he'd just hiked more than seventeen miles with a thirty-five-pound backpack. He ended his message with the upbeat words: "Good livin'."

Daytona 500 winner Bayne revealed in fall 2013 he'd been diagnosed with multiple sclerosis. Doctors cleared the 22-year-old to continue to compete in NASCAR, though. "I am in the best shape I've ever been in, and I feel good," Bayne said. "There are currently no symptoms and I'm committed to continuing to take the best care of my body as possible." He became the youngest driver in NASCAR history to win the Daytona 500 back in 2011.

MS struck country music star Clay Walker in his mid-twenties. At first, he couldn't hold a guitar pick in his right hand or stand. Treatments helped Walker regain use of his right hand and leg—and forge ahead with an active career and a new passion for volunteer work. In more than fifteen years since his diagnosis, Walker has worked tirelessly to raise awareness about multiple sclerosis.

I didn't have fame or superior athleticism. I had determination to try to move in different ways. This is something to note. When you get up and stretch or ride your bike, do you start your routine by asking what you could diversify that day? I can't tell you how empowering it is when you try a different way, a different route. It can be slight, but when you achieve it, what a mental payoff!

One instance of trying a different route happened to start with me falling on the floor. Welcome to my world of common occurrences! I was really struggling to get on my feet from this compromising position. I was as exposed as a person could become in every way. I needed help. That experience would have for many, been humiliating. It didn't feel good for me either, but I came back a champion from this experience. I didn't realize this at the time, but I was sick, and a couple weeks later, I ended up in the hospital with rehab following, in an in-patient PT therapy, for five weeks. I had to learn how to move my body in an entirely different way and come to terms with the wheelchair freeing up more energy from "trying" to walk. Mobility and stability are always the goal, I tell ya! I went from steering a caseload for a major law firm to steering a scooter. In normal times, I stood over six feet tall. Every foot of me falls harder than most people when that connection to my brain stops.

Around the same time, it was eating me up that I couldn't use a fork and knife in the same way anymore. Gone are the days of steak dinners and shots. And my hands shake so much there is no way in hell I would order soup at a restaurant unless everyone at all of the surrounding tables are wearing raincoats! Now, I just needed to nourish my body with the most efficient movement. When I was in the hospital, my physical therapist gave me a go-to method: stabilizing my forearm on an upside bowl to shovel food into my mouth. It's a mechanical action. People watch, and I carry on and smile. A smile that says, *try it sometime, think out of the box.*

It makes me happy that I've had an impact on people through their observations of what living with MS looks like. It's easy to turn away the moment you feel discomforted or challenged by someone going through something that is abnormal. Next time, try not to turn away so quickly. Allow that other person to teach you something positive or forward-moving.

I can't tell you the number of times that my dear friend, Mush Kahn, didn't turn away from me in my hot-mess moments. I know he has learned a great deal: "Trace has made an impact personally and professionally. You hate to compare yourself with someone dealing with MS. But if Trace can deal with that, what am I complaining about? I don't want to say it in any way that puts pity on him. He's been successful at everything he has done and has been goal-oriented. I mean, we are talking MS, which is paralyzing. There are times when he is stuck in his own body, and his ability to push through that and set his own goals is awe-inspiring. He always wanted to talk to other people that had MS, too, but in so that positivity was the topic. He knew some people were in worse situations. His message is, goals may not be a triathlon, but walk the park one day with a cane. A lot of my family members would come up to me and tell me how much they love Trace or the positive influence he is. He truly wants other people in the same boat as him to have the same happiness and positivity. There's probably not a day that goes by that this doesn't motivate me in my life."

With all this talk about crawling on the floor and eating with elbows poised atop a salad bowl, you don't expect me to talk about hiking the Continental Divide (CDT). I'm full of surprises.

Extending 3,100 miles from Canada to Mexico, the CDT encounters a multitude of ecosystems from tundra to desert, hosts a rich variety of wildlife, and preserves nearly two thousand natural, cultural, and historical treasures.

Considered one of the greatest long-distance trails in the world, it is the highest, most challenging, and most remote of National Scenic Trails ranging from 4,000 to 14,000 feet. For the long-distance hiking community (which I am not a member of, in case I've confused you), the CDT is one-third of the "Triple Crown," and annually, while the number is growing, approximately 150 ambitious travelers attempt to complete an end-to-end trek. Parts of the CDT are still in the planning phases, and trail users must bushwhack through, or road walk around, incomplete stretches. Maybe someday. I am not done dreaming!

I spent thirteen years working summers at a Boy Scout camp in the Texas Hill Country . This was the most extraordinary thing, and I guess that I started loving hiking during this immersive time. Also, Shannon and I would go with her entire family to Estes Park, Colorado every summer.

One year, Shannon, her mom, and her sister wanted to go shopping and I asked them to drop me off at the top of the Continental Divide. I would hike up and then straight down. Five of my nephews and nieces said that they wanted to go with me. They were all under 10 years of age. So they did. I remember we made it to the top of the divide and there were about fifty head of elk. They were gawking at us intently, like, what are you doing up here? We also saw lots of marmots. Creatures and beauty surrounded us.

When I contemplate motion, I think about that hike. Exercise consultants say that your body builds up a *movement vocabulary* over time that also aids to performance in certain mental tasks.

I also learned how to wood carve at the CDT. I carved

one Santa that I'm extremely proud of. No pattern. Just what came to mind. He took me thirteen years to finish because I only worked on him when we were on vacation. It got to the point where my hands were shaking so much that I just could not carve, and I was not about to touch his face. Well, I had a brief period of time when the shaking was not bad, and I finished his face. I love staring at him every Christmas!

CHAPTER 7

BETWEEN A WISH AND A GOAL: ACTION!

"The greater the effort, the greater the glory."

—Pierre Corneille

B Y NOW, IT's evident that I push myself ver don't expect accolades. I expect to keep living. A I want to be careful with my message here. If you've lost someone to this disease or any other disease, it doesn't mean that they didn't have grit or didn't fight hard enough.

Early on, I learned that I needed to set goals every day, not just wake up to a new day, and sometimes I was grateful to tears for opening my eyes again, believe me.

Mush clarifies: "Between Trace and Kimi, the family trait is, find your good energy and go get shit done. My parents are from India. I was born in England, moved to the US at 13, been here most of my life. I have worked in Houston since 1990. I've run a variety of companies. I was never without goals exactly. I met the family because I've hired Kimberly's company three or four times. We became friends then met her extended family. Our families are intertwined in many different ways. With Trace setting the example, now every one of us is about, 'find your good energy and go get shit done.'"

Pablo Picasso also talked about getting shit done a little more eloquently: "Our goals can only be reached through a vehicle of a plan, in which we must fervently believe, and upon which we must vigorously act. There is no other route to success."

A TALE OF BOLD GOALS

Nathan Beedle reminded me what bold goals are post-MS. And it's no big revelation, given the man he is. He believes he is more entertaining than me, and I forgive him for that! (I feel compelled to say that he is not.)

As Texas found itself in the midst of a rare and brutal blast of winter weather in February 2021, temperatures plunged below freezing levels, and over 4.3 million people across the state were left without power after high demand for electricity caused the power grid to repeatedly fail. Five days later, snow blanketed everything. People that have lived here for sixty or seventy years have never seen it like this.

In his role, Nathan supervises one hundred prosecutors and twenty-five staff members, the largest group of its kind in Houston. During the storm, some of them had broken pipes and houses that were not functional. With his team comprised of a lot of Texans in their twenties and thirties, they didn't have such adversity or significant life experience to draw on. Nathan held everyone together, and there are particular traits he is equipped with that allowed for work to keep going. A former district attorney with his own practice for a decade, he is a misdemeanor trial bureau chief responsible for about 60,000 misdemeanors a year. You're thinking nerves of steel, right? That is correct. But I want to tell you about his resilience and how he persuaded me to achieve a bold goal.

One day, Nathan showed up at my firm downtown while representing a plaintiff in a case. He was suing one of my doctors. He came to scope out the competition. After we introduced ourselves, we didn't talk about the case at all. We talked about each other, which is not a normal lawyer interaction. Nathan knew I had some condition because he knew the signs of MS from a few friends that had it, but not as severe. Nathan had just participated in a MS run at his daughter's elementary school, too. He was doing his own athletics of triathlons and marathons, he casually mentioned.

My ears perked up. I was wondering how this man with quite a loaded professional life had the time to be so dedicated to training for triathlons and marathons. I realized he was simply dedicated to fitness and tests of endurance, which I needed to tap more into. Low and behold, in that moment, Nathan suggested that I do a sprint triathlon with him. I was wondering if I was having a disease moment of fogginess! He saw my physical state and still challenged me to do a triathlon *and* train with him. Why?

Nathan explains: "It was very organic, and I never use that word. He was not athletic and had never been athletic. He had this debilitating horrible disease that I could tell was already taking him. I felt like, and this is who I am, if I could help give him something to focus on and a goal particularly related to him staying fit as much as he could in his limitations, that would not be harmful as long as we didn't go overboard. I played division one soccer, always been athletic. I lettered in four sports in high school, played division one soccer at the University of Washington. I've run ultra-marathons. I've run marathons. I accomplished stuff I wanted to accomplish and thought he needed something to shoot for out of his comfort zone. I had never done this with someone before. Why are we good friends? 'Sometimes it just works.' It's not something to clearly articulate in words. Sometimes you have to accept where you are in your physical state. Even as an athlete, injuries, pain…how will you come back from it if you can? Trace had never that experience of setting an athletic endeavor for whatever reason. And I felt like, let's see what he says."

My answer? *Wait for it…*

CHAPTER 8

THE BRIGHT LIGHT OF INSPIRATION

"Inspiration exists, but it has to find us working."

—PABLO PICASSO

ES! YEEESSS! WHAT'S the worst that could happen if I set a bold goal? Nathan wouldn't force me to keep going if I was clearly dying during the training, right? I accepted the challenge immediately. Call me crazy. It's not the first time.

In 2010, I started working out seven days a week for the first time in my life. I still work out seven days a week. Don't think Incredible Hulk-type workouts but Trace-type workouts. I work with a PT twice a week and work out the other five days. I have to. You must beat the odds however you humanly can.

Training for the sprint triathlon brought a group of wonderful people into my life. If I had known that being a jock would bring so many lifelong friends, I may have picked up a dumbbell much sooner!

I started working with the fabulous personal trainer, Trisha Bicknell at Villa Sport. You have to establish trust in people who care for your health like personal trainers, doctors, and psychologists, and I trusted Trisha instantly. By this time, I'm sure she is even more credentialed up as a corrective exercise specialist, medical exercise specialist and flexibility coach. I approached her in all my display of MS with the bold goal of training for a triathlon. She did not laugh but worked with me to strengthen my core muscles in both the front and back.

Funny story: We used to do little fun runs and stuff as training for the triathlon. Well, Trisha was trying to work with me on my core. She referred to my posture as my 'attitude'. We were walking on this evening walk surrounded by a large group of people and she screamed, "Your attitude sucks!" She was meaning that I was not standing up straight, but everyone around us was gawking at her like, how could this horrible woman scream at this man with walking sticks and obviously having trouble.

Soon, in the locker room, Super Ironman Jim Harrington had heard me interacting with others as my upbeat self. Amazingly, he had just completed the MS 150 from Houston to Austin. One thing you get when you finish is a lapel pin and T-shirt. One morning, Jim actually put those items in his duffel bag to work out and presented them to me, saying, "I've heard you talking about having MS. I just completed the MS 150 and I'd like you to have these to know we care and are trying to understand this." Who knows if he expected tears from me in the locker room loaded down with jocks, but he got them anyway. We became fast friends. Jim has completed twelve Ironman competitions, 30+ halves, and 60+ marathons.

Despite his incredible workload, Nathan patiently walked with me every Sunday morning at 5:00 a.m. I used walking sticks. I could not walk fifty feet the first time. It took me a few months to do three and a half miles; Jim says I have a "crappy body and an incredible mind!" What Jim has been able to do with his body is profound, but we've learned a lot from each other. When we met, I was using a cane and had been scheduled for a chair. With encouragement by Nathan and Jim, I began riding a bike a lot more. They set me up with a training station at home. I kept it in my mind that exercising prolongs life. I had cancelled the wheelchair and for the next five or six years, I got by without it. Nathan and Jim didn't treat me any differently for having MS. Instead, they constantly tried to imagine what all this would be like. The inabilities. When we did train, they didn't make excuses for me.

In training for the sprint triathlon, two elements I had to contend for in my mind were the heat, which would inevitably cause me to short-circuit, and the biking portion, which would be extremely difficult. I didn't get bottled up with fear though. I had so much support; I wouldn't forgive myself for just crumbling and wasting their time.

People quickly found out that I was doing the sprint triathlon. A bunch of high school kids, my super jocks, and then lawyers, doctors, housewives, signed up to join me. What a feeling!

On those days that I was low on energy and motivation, I looked to inspiration from guys like Nathan and Jim, and how disciplined and dedicated they are. Jim had worked for Shell Oil, which transferred him to Houston, with a two-hour commute. When he stopped working for Shell and went to work for a private pipeline company, which freed up two hours that he spent on conditioning his body. He had a friend, a triathlete, who started meeting him at the YMCA for a spin class and encouraged him to do his first triathlon. The pursuit of more competitions just built from there. He picked up a private coach when he achieved Ironman level. So, he does several of these big competitions per year, plus a sprint marathon every month. It takes a long time to condition your body and your mind to reach that Ironman level. It's not something you just walk into. …Or is it?

I offered a job to Scott Riddle, who had just graduated

from law school and was a former baseball player for the University of Arkansas. I had my feet on my messy desk when he walked in. He eyed me and the orange cat in my lap, with pure amusement. Regardless of what you think would be appropriate questions for a new lawyer, I asked Scott three questions: Do you swim? Do you bike? Do you run? When he responded in the affirmative, then I told him, "Great, you are on my triathlon team!" He walked into an upcoming triathlon and a new position. I immediately hired him! It's funny to think of our first meeting (and his impression), given that we're the best of friends today. We didn't talk about traditional things of law school. I wanted to get to know his personality and passions. I had started this firm with two partners, and we built it into an honorable force, defending doctors. But I was struggling physically, and I couldn't hide it from Scott. I sensed a lot of empathy, pure heart, from this man, and I didn't feel embarrassed though I was *supposed* to have this air of a debonair, brilliant trial attorney with this young man's fate in my hands.

Have you ever noticed that some people can truly hold themselves together even when they are nervous? You don't see shaking limbs, twitches. They are literally holding themselves together. If you pay close attention, you may see the anxiety in their body language below the waist (not that!), as they shift from one foot to the other or stamp their foot hard into the carpet to relieve the tension within. In addition, some people's faces turn red—and that can't be prevented (says my Irish co-writer). With MS, there is no disguising some of the symptoms as the disease escalates. Imbalance, facial pain, muscle spasms, electrical pain stabbing you in various areas. You can't grit your teeth and move on. You get to a point when you can no longer hold yourself together. Your body creates its own public display for all to see. And I still smoked cigarettes for some time, which probably presented me as a twitching male version of Betty Davis!

Scott had been among the first people to see me in my authentic state of illness and attempting to maintain my professional life. That cemented our bond. I had to disband from the firm shortly after we met. He sensed this was imminent. Nevertheless, I needed friends like him to weather bigger storms. I am extremely proud to say that I continue to mentor Scott today and he is now the partner of an extremely prestigious law firm in Dallas. Scott got married to someone much better than him (*ha-ha*), Reagan, three years ago in New Orleans. Kimi, Michael, my mother and I all traveled to New Orleans from Houston in a big van to celebrate their wedding. It was a wonderful time for all. My mother especially loved it.

Today, Scott's practice revolves around crash accidents and general transportation events. In fact, he works with a fascinating expert who is responsible for investigating the highest-altitude plane crash in history where he had to hike a mountain with a team to investigate. How could I compete with that?

Another star of my team, which eventually morphed into Team Inspiration, is Brandon Loughridge, who played high school basketball with my son. He didn't know me at the time, but he had heard a group of guys talking about training for Team Inspiration. He would go on to do an

Ironman in my name, with his college roommate, Tyler Blanton. I got to stand at the Iron Man finish line and hang their metals on them. It was a highlight of my life. They raised $15,000 for the MS Society. When it comes to training, Brandon tries to tackle all three events, swimming, running and biking, once a week. (Today, I think he ran fifteen miles!) With Brandon and Tyler being like sons to me, I've tried to teach them to never be a victim of circumstances. In their high school years, they saw me train for an event I wasn't "supposed" to be doing, and this pushed them more. Brandon says he will never forget seeing me crossing the bridge 'on my last leg' long after the race shut down! Both Brandon and Tyler will tell you that image encouraged them to train after a full day of school and other activities.

"This is the first time I thought about why," said Tyler. "Why we train, why we roll, why we compete. Seeing Trace at the Ironman finish line has stuck with me. I would be in the middle of a run and find myself thinking about him. He struggled, but that is not what I remember most."

TRIATHLON DAY—SAY WHAT?

In completing in a sprint triathlon, I wasn't trying to emulate anyone. It was a mental challenge. Can I get my leg to cooperate for an event of this magnitude? It was that simple. I didn't think about anything else leading up to the big event. It helps to know that forty or fifty people could just call it a day, pick me up and carry me back to my TV set! But I wasn't going out like that.

One of the most memorable things for me is that every Sunday, Nathan and I would walk. Rain or fog, it didn't matter. Every time we walked, we would see a gentleman riding a bike with one leg. He had a prosthesis on the other leg. The week before the triathlon, they always have a practice swim in Lake Woodlands where the competition would be. I did the practice and then I just happened to be walking under a flagpole on a point on the lake when I met Chris. I said, "Seeing you riding that bike every week made me say to myself, 'if he can do this triathlon, so can I.'" He looked at me, smiling, and said, "That's funny, every time I saw you walking, I said the same thing to myself."

Nathan describes the scene, as so much is blurry to me, and I don't think I could do it justice. "I was entered, and I shadowed him in the swim to make sure he was okay. The swimming part is the most dangerous for anybody usually. I grew up swimming competitively, played water polo. I treaded water to make sure he was okay. But the most dangerous for Trace was the bike. If his legs started to act up or he lost motor control, he was going to go down and it wouldn't be pretty. That portion of it, I was most concerned about. Once we got through that, I knew we would make it. It may have taken several hours and many, many breaks. The heat of the day had increased significantly. His body tends to shut down with heat. With swelling of nervous system, spine, swelling of 'Jarvis', the bad leg, which had a habit of not cooperating even on cold days. I was really anxious, and he was fully concentrated on making it. The course had long been shut down and picked up by the time we finished. He was beyond spent. There is something about your excrement system. For a certain prolonged activity, it kicks up for more activity for all athletes, and I don't think his body had ever gone there. We were lucky there was a port o'can at the 1.5-mile mark of the race, so we were able to deal with it. He was embarrassed, but it's happened to me, too. That is a sign of an athlete." *Oh man, Nathan had the audacity to call me an athlete!*

"He had gotten through the swim, crashed on the bike but got through, then the run was going to be the most difficult. It was a very hot day. He had a personal trainer at the health club. Several of us were there and just believed in him. He took off on this 3.1-mile run and it took hours and hours for him to get through it. Someone went and got energy gels. Others brought ice and water. All the vendors were gone, the finish line was gone, and this group of people just stayed to help. Here, I just want to convey the magnitude of his humility: When his body was so taxed, short-circuiting big time, his speech was slurred, he was dehydrated. I would have gone and hid in the bushes and told everyone to go away. He lost his bowels. We went to a construction port o-potty. We helped clean him up. I mean, I would have been horrified. He didn't want it, didn't deserve it, but he endured it. It shows that he has drive and motivation that surpasses most people. I don't care if you can do a marathon, you wouldn't persevere under those conditions.

"The best part of it was the race was over. We enter the park and reach the bridge. They had taken a banner, tied it to the railing of the bridge, where the finish line was that had long since been gone, they put it across the sidewalk and his mother was there holding it. His mother hugged him and the first thing she said was, 'I'm so proud of you'. He not only perseveres, but he makes life better for those around him."

I need to emphasize the part about my mom being there at the finish line. Another bold goal, seriously, and a testament to who my mother was. She had just been diagnosed with melanoma the summer before. She was so freckly, so I don't know how they found it! Kimi was taking her to this appointment then lunch, but it turned out to be the whole day. It was a little sobering. No fun things! As she went into surgery, Kimi had to warn the doctors and nurse that Mom doesn't complain at all; if she says she isn't feeling well, pay attention. She came out of surgery and the doctors said they needed Kimi because Mom "wasn't feeling well." Well, according to Kimi, she was grey! She said her chest had pressure and was nauseated, back pain. They did an EKG, which looked normal. Then cardiac enzymes. Normal. It was like a rapid medical thriller the way my sister describes it.

She was grey and weird. She was looking at Kimi, pretty blue eyes normally, but from one dot of melanoma, her arm had been cut wrist to elbow! So maybe she had a slight heart attack? She stayed a few days. Her enzymes were positive after 48 hours—she needed a double bypass! Friday for melanoma; Monday, heart catheter; and then that Friday, double bypass. That was a horrible round for her. Mom was moved into a rehabilitation facility to help her continue to gain strength from her open heart surgery on July 4th weekend. Upon admitting her, everyone noticed Mom was retaining a lot of fluid and having severe stomach issues.

After running some tests, she tested positive for C. diff. We called the hospital back since she caught this severe bacteria in the hospital and they re-admitted her for another two weeks to clear the infection and ensure the heart was okay through this ordeal. That was how my mom spent her summer, so to be on the course with me the following spring was truly a gift.

For the walk portion of the sprint triathlon, a large group, including my sister and niece, Emerson, did it with me. The police stayed on the course, even though everyone else had finished. They were holding me up, icing me down with the help of people in houses. The police kept clearing the cars because I was still an "active runner." In a burst of determination/desperation, I ran through the ribbon. My mom, who fought her own health battle just eight months prior, was at the finish line with the biggest smile on her face I had ever seen.

I had trained for a year for a sprint triathlon, and this achievement started with setting a bold goal. I dreamed out loud and a lot of people had heard me and supported that dream.

Nathan adds: "I've been around a lot of talented athletes in my life. People with incredible physiques, people that played in NFL for eight years as running backs. But none of their hearts were a tenth of what Trace Sherer was able to get out of his frame. It's straight motivation, perseverance, intensity. He's such a great person, but he has really fought this disease so strongly. If I could just give my employees or my children ten percent of his heart. My dad was a good athlete but not great, and what made him good was his heart and how hard he worked. You will never outwork my dad at anything. It left a mark on me. Trace had so many roadblocks, walls, but he pushed them aside. I deal with a lot of people. Meet with defendants nearly every day and their lawyers going through bad things. You can tell who a good person is, a quality person, and I don't think there is a higher person than I've ever met than Trace. You don't get to choose the hand you are dealt in some circumstances. Trace did not choose to have this horrible disease. The question is how you are going to respond to this thing that is now a part of your life. Some people shut it down and some people continue on for twenty years when your diagnosis is that you should have passed in one. That is amazing. That is attributed to perseverance, heart, moving forward. Slower pace maybe, but still moving forward."

One of the most incredible and beautiful moments of this story included Shannon, my ex-wife. She did not come to the race, but when it was done though she came to my house. I was worthless and lying on the cold tile floor. She came in, got on the ground, put her arm around me and said, "I'm so proud of you."

We laid in silence for a long time. Then she started laughing hysterically. I said, "What the hell are you laughing about?"

She said, "I just had a horrible realization. How the hell are the two of us going to get up from here?" She was wearing a wig by this time due to her loss of hair from chemotherapy and was dying of cancer. We had been divorced for a decade. But damn, I think we laughed harder together than we did in our marriage.

Through this entire journey that started with setting a bold goal and drawing from the power of inspiration, Tyler and Brandon have become two of my best friends. In May of 2015, they finished the Ironman in my name. I was sitting on a restaurant patio viewing the race. By this time, it was impossible to put my body through anything that remotely signified what I had done years before. I can tell you that those supporting Team Inspiration on the sidelines were the loudest, most spirited group by a landslide when Brandon and Tyler crossed the finish line. It was a really inspiring spectacle to see.

Do not let anyone tell you that you cannot do something. Do not even tell yourself that.

Team Inspiration Texas went on to fulfill other bold goals, such as raising money through other competitions to fight Duchenne muscular dystrophy and ovarian cancer.

Then Jim and Scott got this crazy idea to do a race on Cinco de Mayo.

The race was open. They dressed up in sombreros and put me in a wheelbarrow, pretty much laughing the whole time. They pushed me through the streets of Dallas in a wheelbarrow, providing great entertainment to the traffic police on every corner. All the girls wanted to jump in the wheelbarrow with me and have their picture taken. Never thought this could attract the girls! They didn't care that the wheels were falling off. My signature prop became a blue wig for Team Inspiration's dodge ball tournament. Who gets to be so lucky to have these memories?

CHAPTER 9

KISS THE SKY...AND OTHER JOYS

"Don't be scared to fly high because it will inspire others."

—*KERLI*

You've probably gathered by now that not using the word "can't" already increases my moments in life. Well, I had every excuse to say "can't" to skydiving when it was presented to me by my son, Trevor.

Skydive Monroe based in Atlanta, states, "The reason people skydive has a lot more to do with celebrating life than it does with defying death. ... Skydiving is probably the most empowering thing you'll ever do in your life, hands-down. Once you do it, you'll be changed forever. After all, you'll know that you can face the scariest situation imaginable–more than 10,000 feet of empty air yawning wide open between you and the ground!–and literally laugh (okay: scream-laugh) in its face. The superpowers you discover up there will change the way you look at literally every other challenge in your life."

Pretty persuasive words!

My son had gone skydiving and offered it as a birthday present. I initially said, "Uh, no!" Then something overcame me, prompting me to do this. It was the most enriching and extraordinary thing that I've ever done. First, I ended up in the hospital unexpectedly. While in the hospital, I needed to dream out loud. I needed a positive focus for when I was going to get out. I started sharing my dream with anyone who would listen—doctors, nurses, physical therapists, family, and friends. It took me two months of recovering from pneumonia, but I enticed a group of first-timers and suited up to jump from 13,000 feet.

One of those people was my friend, Richard Hubscher. I hired him to walk my dog while I was in the hospital for a month. When I asked him to join me for skydiving, he looked at me like I was an alien. He recalls, "I thought, he is never going to get out of the hospital! Skydiving…what in the world?"

You see, Richard still walks my dog three times a day. As such, he is my captive audience as I work through my Random Thoughts videos to share with others. I will share his story here, too, because if you had picked out in a crowd who had suggested skydiving, you would have guessed the other! I illustrated Richard's inspirational story in a recent post: "People are more likely to encourage or support you when you are earnestly fulfilling your dream. Sometimes you don't know where that support comes from. He was dyslexic and had a horrible time in school. He was heading down a dark and dangerous path. Fortunately, like me, he has an amazing sister, who encouraged his interest. In 1977, he saw Mikhail Baryshnikov and fell in love with the artistry and athleticism of ballet, so he started studying it. Richard has been with the Houston Ballet for more than forty years. He's been to a performance of the Royal Ballet with the queen. He has danced for three Presidents. He has danced on the Great Wall of China. Positive people are glass half-full kind of people. Every time we do something toward our dream, we fill our glass a little fuller. When someone else is supporting us, they too fill our glass. Before you know it, your cup will overfloweth!"

With at least a glass half full of encouragement and people like Richard behind me, I snapped into a major recovery and went skydiving. It was a fantastic experience. Richard says that as soon as he jumped, he was just anxious to reach the ground, but as soon as he hit the ground, he wanted to go again.

Once you jump, it's silence and beauty, nothing else.

One of the biggest misconceptions about skydiving is that you hang onto an instructor for dear life and go where the wind carries you both. Not exactly. Maintaining a certain body position in freefall and picking up your legs for landing is essential. Knowing that was scary for someone who doesn't have full range of motion or full control of their limbs. Fear is not an absolute, however. Do you know what treats fear? Breathing. That's right, breathing. Fortunately, we went to Skydive Spaceland whose staff understood my physical limitations and actually caught me as I was landing.

I'm happy to report that Richard said he thinks of us skydiving when he just wants to sit on his butt. Not dancing on the Great Wall of China but skydiving with me! Crazy Town.

Three years ago, I did a speaking engagement on "getting off your ass and moving" basically, but I started to have more trouble traveling and taking care of myself in between gigs. When I was first diagnosed with MS, someone gave me a poster with author and artist Mary Anne Radmacher's quote, "Courage does not always roar. Sometimes courage is the quiet voice at the end of the day saying, 'I will try again tomorrow.'" My speech was about trying. Just try. Today, you can walk five steps. Tomorrow, walk six. The next day, more. Who cares how long it may take you? Kindergarteners reached voting age by the time it took me to finish the triathlon! I can try everything. Including skydiving.

With the skydiving venture, I created an experience for people who otherwise would not have had it. I helped them expand their own horizons. It's still pure joy when I think about that day. Where do you elicit joy? When times are tough, don't forget.

HUMANS HAVE A NEUROLOGICAL RESPONSE TO ANIMALS

Another joy is my pets. What a key to my mental health! If you're at all able to get a pet, do. I have always had animals around me in my life, but I did not realize how incredibly important they are at this particular stage. I need to tell you a little bit about my fur kids. When I was married and my kids were little, we had several magnificent animals. As time went by, they grew up old and happy. But they got sick. In the same year, I had to put all three of my pets to sleep. That literally killed me. At some point in our lives, we ended up with a cat, as well as the dogs. The one cat that I had was my son's and her name was Twinkles. Long story. Another book!

One of my dear friends is a cat veterinarian. A week after she put my last animal down, she called me and told me she had a new cat for me. I was not interested at all. She told me to at least come and meet this cat. I did, fell in love, and took her home. She must've been abused because she is incredibly shy. The only human that has been allowed to touch her has been me. Recently, six years later, she has finally allowed Richard and one of my friends to touch her. Otherwise, she hides under the bed when anyone else is around. But she's awesome.

A year after that, I went to Dallas for a wedding. I was at the reception. There may have been some alcohol involved.

My dear friend called me and asked if my cat could have a friend. Her friend was in the bank parking lot and a kitten jumped into her engine. The kitten maybe was a month old. I said absolutely not. Of course, I have that cat now, too.

A year later, that same friend asked me to help her with a pet adoption at my apartment. I told her absolutely not. Of course, I did and the first dog that was brought in jumped in my lap, kissed me, and has never left my side. He's honestly the most awesome dog I have ever owned. I was reluctant to get a dog, as walking was such a difficulty, but I had three neighbors that came up to me at the pet adoption and said that if I found a dog that I liked, they would walk him. And they did. It was remarkable.

Upon living in the city, I hired Richard, who has become a wonderful friend. Richard loves my pets as much as I do. He also administers my shots three times a week and my eye drops nightly. With my pets came a nurse who has danced for three U.S. Presidents. Life is truly a wonder.

CHAPTER 10

YOU ARE WHO YOU LEAVE BEHIND

"People who are truly strong lift others up. People who are truly powerful bring others together."

—MICHELLE OBAMA

M Y MOTHER ALWAYS produced the eggs Benedict every New Year's Day. It really was a production. When we got older, we started doing eggs Benedict every Easter. My grandmother had a recipe for what is the best hollandaise sauce in the world. Seriously. Because of the cast of dozens of guests we would always include, including Team Inspiration, we would operate a huge assembly line with different people toasting English muffins, poaching eggs, etc. But I was in charge of the hollandaise sauce. If it was slightly off, I was livid. So I became a drill sergeant when it had anything to do with my sauce. Scott and Jim spent Easters with us, so they were part of the line! They knew they would rue the day if they messed with my sauce. If I reacted badly, one of them would distract me with a picture of the shake weight, a silly gift they gave me for my birthday one year, that contains goofy pictures like one featuring Burt Reynolds or of me in the blue wig.

I have received so much from every single person I have acknowledged in my story about cultivating nerves of steel. I have tried to implant my legacy of positivity in my central world.

My son, Trevor, said of this central world: "Part of my life is knowing how I want to live my life since my parents couldn't fully live theirs. Something I try not to think about, but it creeps in my mind all the time—my dad lost his legs, diagnosed at 32. I turn 30 tomorrow. Last hours of my twenties! I'm very empathetic, so I just feel so bad for my dad. I feel his positive outlook on life and him generally accepting his fate and how to get beyond it. I can never have any excuses. Do things as urgently as "yesterday" if you want to do them because you may not have the opportunity tomorrow. Kimi is one of my mentors. Mush and Michael are as well. I call them about everything I need help with from life perspective. They are the first people I talk to. After working in corporate media, Kimi started her first company coaching executives and helping C-level executives strategize their business to help align talent to deliver better performance and change the way companies operate, think outside the box. The way she has been able to pivot I just find so interesting. I hope it has come across that my dad is an amazing person. The community of people that are willing to help him are truly dedicated to him. He is magnetic, inspiring. You have no reason to complain. Sometimes you are dealt the short stick, but you have to make the most of it."

Mush concurs: "I've learned that bravery is not just happy and jolly and inspirational. It's struggling mightily physically and emotionally and being resilient from those low points and be willing to find a way to contribute. Many people have a barrier, and it takes over their life. No matter what, find a place back to dreaming out loud. I admire that tremendously. I want my two sons, 18 and 20, to live this."

CHAPTER 11

RUN ON EMPTY OR RUN ON ATTITUDE

*"Knowledge is not a passion from without the mind,
but an active exertion of the inward strength, vigor
and power of the mind, displaying itself from within."*

—RALPH CUDWORTH

NEVER GIVE UP. I could have quit in 1999 and here we are in 2021. I'm writing and fighting. This applies to every area in life. Whether it's your marriage, your job, training physically, the hectic aspects of life, don't give up. In whatever you do, do it to the best of your ability. Make that effort lifelong.

Don't let MS or any other disease define you. Lynn's mother also has MS. She is quite a fighter. She doesn't let this disease shove her down. She doesn't walk either. She's in a scooter. She was diagnosed late in life. She can get on a walker and walk a few steps to get around her kitchen or something and she has had it longer than me. We both need assistance, but she does a little better without physical therapy. It shows how the disease works. I'm on meds, and Lynn's mother stopped taking meds seven years ago. She also knows to be around positive people. There is enough going on in the world to remind you of the negative or challenging. Find the positives.

So many people who I knew with MS are indeed, dead. Then my ex-wife died from breast cancer. My youngest son's friend's mother had MS, and I watched her go from leaning on a cane, to a walker, and then gone.

Shannon had a hard time being positive in the face of tragedy. In her mind, I was dead once I got this diagnosis. I set out to be a happy, positive individual despite how terrified I was sometimes, despite everyone else's pain seeing my deterioration. I also helped her see the light of positivity. It may take time to help someone else see the light of positivity. Whether for you or someone else, keep devoting time to carving that light out. In a meaningful life, light is synonymous with breath.

We rush through life so much. We have packed schedules. There is a certain frenetic pace to life especially here in America. I used to live that way until a debilitating disease slowed me down considerably. I've learned that there is a lot of life packed into *this moment*. We could all use that reminder to be present and slow down—and to show us what courage really looks like. Courage is when you are devastated, emotionally, physically, and you are willing to eke out the small victory that no one else is going to see. There is tremendous honor in that, says the happy hiker and skydiver.

What are your small victories? What motivates you to get to the next moment? Instead of fixing a shortcoming, develop a strength. Remember that even the scary act of falling can jolt you from the mundane of just getting by and illuminate a new path for discovery or a new challenge that you can conquer. Not only will you find your nerves of steel. Your dream may be revealed in these trying times.

I dreamed of doing a triathlon. Done. I dreamed of writing a book. Done. I guess it is time to start dreaming again! Dream with me.

REFERENCES

Interviews by Author

Nathan Beedle. Phone interview. February 18, 2020.

Tyler Blanton. Phone interview. June 29, 2020.

Kimberly Cutchall. 1) Phone interview. September 1, 2020. 2) Zoom interview. September 19, 2020.

Jim Harrington. Phone interview. July 23, 2020.

Mush Khan. 1) Phone interview. August 28, 2020. 2) Zoom interview. September 19, 2020.

Brandon Loughridge. Phone interview. November 30, 2020.

Lynn Maki. Phone interview. October 2, 2020.

Scott Riddle. Phone interview. July 2, 2020.

Barbara Sherer. Zoom interview. September 19, 2020.

Trevor Sherer. Phone interview. July 1, 2020.

Publications

Bridges, Frances. "5 Ways to Be A More Positive Person." *Forbes.* March 29, 2019.

https://www.forbes.com/sites/francesbridges/2019/03/29/5-ways-to-be-a-more-positive-person/?sh=59ebc8bb716d

Felson, Sabrina, MD (reviewed by). "Famous Faces of Multiple Sclerosis." *WebMD.* August 1, 2019.

https://www.webmd.com/multiple-sclerosis/ss/slideshow-faces-of-ms

Free Patents Online. "Heat exchange tube insertion tool: United States Patent 4831720."

https://www.freepatentsonline.com/4831720.html

John Hopkins Medicine. "The Power of Positive Thinking."

https://www.hopkinsmedicine.org/health/wellness-and-prevention/the-power-of-positive-thinking

The Neurology Center. "Multiple Sclerosis."

https://www.theneurologycenter.com/services/multiple-sclerosis/

Robinson, Dan. "How the 1989 Exxon Valdez oil spill unfolded and its impact on the energy industry." *NS Energy.* June 5, 2020.

https://www.nsenergybusiness.com/features/exxon-valdez-oil-spill-1989/

Sherer, Trace. "Beating MS; Trace keeps Dreaming Out Loud." *Blogspot.com.* August 14, 2015-February 25, 2015.

http://tracesherer.blogspot.com/2014/

Sparks, Hannah. "Joe DiMeo, face and hand transplant recipient, reveals historic results." *New York Post*. February 3, 2021.

https://nypost.com/2021/02/03/face-and-hand-transplant-recipient-steps-out-for-the-first-time/

Tolson, Michelle. "What I'd Tell Someone with a New MS Diagnosis." National MS Society. December 17, 2020.

https://www.healthline.com/health/multiple-sclerosis/what-id-tell-someone-with-a-new-ms-diagnosis

Walk, Jon. "Sherer, diagnosed with MS, set for CB&I." *Houston Chronicle*. May 4, 2011.

https://www.chron.com/neighborhood/woodlands/sports/article/Sherer-diagnosed-with-MS-set-for-CB-I-9349105.php

ABOUT THE AUTHORS

Trace J. Sherer is an attorney and mediator who has been living (and thriving) with MS for more than twenty years. *Nerves of Steel* is his debut as an author. He lives in Houston with two diva cats and one dog. Trace is working on his second book, a legal thriller. He loves to hear from readers. Contact him at trace@nervesofsteel.org.

Candi S. Cross is the founder of You Talk I Write, a modern ghostwriting agency. She has co-developed approximately 140 books with authors worldwide. Candi is committed to helping diverse individuals with contemporary stories that make a difference. She lives in New York City with her wife and 24/7 muse, Liza. For more info, visit *www.youtalkiwrite.com.*